NAVAJO RUG DESIGNS

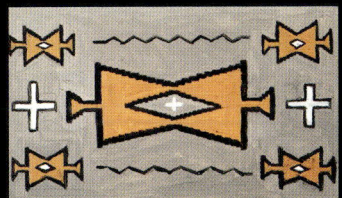

ACKNOWLEDGMENTS

Many thanks to the entire National Park Service staff at Hubbell Trading Post National Historic Site, including Ed Chamberlin, Kathleen Tabaha, Nancy Stone, and volunteer John Vinck. I am also very grateful to Ann Lane Hedlund and Martha Blue for their generous assistance.

—S.L.

Rio Nuevo Publishers®
P.O. Box 5250, Tucson, Arizona 85703-0250
(520) 623-9558, www.rionuevo.com

Text © 2005 by Susan Lowell. All rights reserved. No part of this book may be reproduced, stored, introduced into a retrieval system, or otherwise copied in any form without the prior written permission of the publisher, except for brief quotations in reviews or citations.

Design: Karen Schober, Seattle, Washington
Front cover: Hubbell Trading Post image HUTR 3522; back cover: HUTR 3523.

Library of Congress Cataloging-in-Publication Data
Lowell, Susan, 1950-
  Navajo rug designs / Susan Lowell.
    p. cm. — (Look West series)
Includes bibliographical references.
ISBN-13 978-1-887896-72-6 (hardcover); ISBN 1-887896-72-4 (hardcover)
 1. Navajo textile fabrics—History. 2. Navajo textile fabrics—Themes, motives. 3. Navajo blankets—Themes, motives. 4. Hubbell, John Lorenzo—Private collections. 5. Hubbell Trading Post National Historic Site (Ganado, Ariz.)—Ethnological collections. I. Title. II. Series: Look West.
  E99.N3L793 2005
  746.7'2'041—dc22

2005003833

Printed in Hong Kong
10 9 8 7 6 5 4 3 2 1

NAVAJO RUG DESIGNS

Susan Lowell

PHOTOGRAPHY BY Robin Stancliff

LOOK WEST
SERIES

RIO NUEVO PUBLISHERS
TUCSON, ARIZONA

JUST LOOK AT THEM. LOOK QUICKLY,

AND THE VIVID STRIPES, ZIGZAGS, AND DIAMONDS WILL

DAZZLE YOUR EYES. LOOK SLOWLY, AND NOTICE THE OPTICAL

ILLUSIONS. CATCH THE RHYTHMS, BOTH SIMPLE AND COMPLEX.

AND LOOK AT THE INTERPLAY OF BLACK AND WHITE

WITH RED, YELLOW, AND BLUE; THE JOYFUL BALANCE;

THE INTELLIGENCE; THE BEAUTY.

These 102 classic Navajo designs (and three Hopi ones) come from the art collection of the Hubbell Trading Post in Ganado, Arizona, which has been a center of Native American art and commerce ever since the 1870s. Most of the photographs in this book don't show actual weavings. Instead they reproduce paintings, drawings, and silkscreen prints of rugs and blankets. But the designs did play an important role in the development of Navajo weaving. As early as 1914 George Wharton James admired them in *Indian Blankets and Their Makers*:

> In his office at Ganado, Arizona, John Lorenzo Hubbell has scores of blanket designs, painted in oil, hung upon the walls, and they present a most surprising and wonderful combination. These are designs that have been found to be pleasing to purchasers, and when a special order for a blanket of a certain design comes in, the weaver is shown the picture of the one desired. She studies it a while ... and then, with such slight variations as she is sure to introduce, goes ahead and makes her blanket.

Each of these patterns makes a strong, complete statement without

Portrait of J. L. Hubbell, 1908. E. A. Burbank, Conté crayon on paper.

using a single word. Words can suggest, especially words like "banners," "butterflies," "color music," and "visual feast." But in the end, all that language can do is help to locate the images in space and time. Wordlessly, straight to the mind and senses, the designs speak about human history, passion, faith, and fun. To communicate fully, they must be seen, and happily here they are.

A weaver shows her rug to J. L. Hubbell, seated in front of his trading post. Other weavings in the background resemble the painted rug designs. Photo by Ben Wittick, c. 1895.

| NAVAJO RUG DESIGNS |

Described in the voluminous Hubbell papers as rug or blanket "studies" and "sketches" as well as pictures, paintings, and designs, the images date from the late 1890s to the 1930s. The underlying textile designs are older, dating back to about 1850. Though many of

ABOVE: *Two unidentified men in Hubbell's office, decorated with framed rug designs, c. 1910.*
RIGHT: *Rugs for sale at Hubbell Trading Post, 2005.*

these designs have influenced Navajo weaving for a century—especially the early twentieth-century phase often called the Hubbell Revival—most of them have never been published before. Nor have they ever appeared as a set.

Probably each painted image is based on a real textile, and in fact some of the models still exist. And so do thousands of weavings that

they have influenced over the last hundred years. The daughters, granddaughters, and great-granddaughters, so to speak, of these designs have helped to spread fine Navajo weaving throughout the world. To catch the look of woven wool, the graphic artists used a wide range of media, including oil, watercolor, gouache, tempera, silkscreen, ink, crayon, and pencil on paper, board, and canvas. The average size is about 8 x 10 inches, though a few examples are twice as large, and a few are merely snapshot-sized. We know the names of at least

E. A. Burbank, c. 1905.

eight painters who contributed to this extraordinary gallery of designs. But some of the artists remain anonymous, and so do all of the weavers, unfortunately.

Elbridge Ayer Burbank painted the largest number of pictures (32), followed by Bertha Little (18), Hardesty Gillmore Maratta (4), Raymond Pearson (3), Waldo Mootzka (2), and Herbert Bolivar Judy or Tschudy (1). The remaining images are unsigned, except for Louis Ewing's portfolio of fifteen silkscreen prints. Not all of the pictures are framed, and only a portion of the collection ever actually

hung on Hubbell's wall. Some of them have been lost, too. But about forty paintings remain on display in the rug room of the trading post, which is still in operation as a National Historic Site.

Rug room decorated with framed rug designs, 2005.

| NAVAJO RUG DESIGNS |

The original collector, and in most cases the commissioner, of the artwork was John, also called Juan, Lorenzo Hubbell (1853–1930), an early trader to Native Americans and an influential figure in the history of Navajo weaving. The trilingual, multicultural Hubbell was born in New Mexico Territory to a Spanish-American mother and a Yankee father. Throughout his long, adventurous life he played many parts: entrepreneur, politician, sheriff, rancher, open-handed host, wheeler-dealer, family man, and Don Juan. To the Navajos he was first known as *Nák'ee sinilí* (Double Glasses or Man Wearing Spectacles) and then

Naakaii Sání (Old Mexican). Theodore Roosevelt, one of many famous visitors attracted to remote Ganado, supposedly nicknamed Hubbell "Lorenzo the Magnificent"—a reference to his role as patron of the arts as well as *patrón* of a substantial hacienda. Like the Medici, the Hubbell family combined strong business sense with a genuine eye for beauty, and J. L. Hubbell's taste certainly shines in the rug paintings. Yet he is only one factor in their story.

At first glance a Navajo loom seems a simple matter of sticks and strings. But everything to do with Navajo weaving is packed with paradox and far from simple. Is it a craft or an art? The answer is both. Is it a women's or a men's activity? Same answer: although most weavers are female, there have always been a few men, too. Is Navajo weaving ancient and traditional or modern, individualistic, and innovative? Is it distinctively Navajo or shaped by outside influences? Do weavers work for love or money? Are Navajo textiles beautiful or useful?

| NAVAJO RUG DESIGNS |

Long ago Spider Woman,

a Holy Person,

instructed the Navajo women

how to weave on a loom

which Spider Man told them how to make.

The crosspoles were made of sky and earth cords,

the warp sticks of sun rays,

the healds of rock crystal and sheet lightning.

The batten was a sun halo, white shell made the comb.

There were four spindles;

one a stick of zigzag lightning with a whorl of cannel coal;

one a stick of flash lightning with a whorl of turquoise;

a third had a stick of sheet lightning with a whorl of abalone;

a rain streamer formed the stick of the fourth,

and its whorl was white shell.

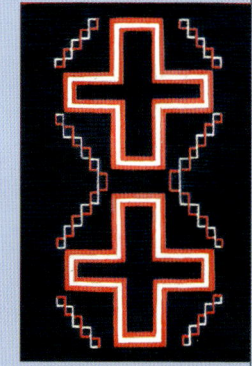

—Adapted from a Navajo legend quoted in
SPIDER WOMAN: A STORY OF NAVAJO WEAVERS AND CHANTERS
by Gladys A. Reichard
(New York: Macmillan, 1934)

Primitive or sophisticated? Blankets or rugs? To all of these rather simplistic questions the answer is: both, and that's only the beginning.

Religious tradition explains Navajo weaving as a gift of great power and value bestowed by two Holy People, Spider Woman and Spider Man. Tool-making Spider Man is said to have created the loom, batten, comb, and spindle from potent natural forces such as lightning, sunshine, and rain, and special treasures such as white shell and turquoise.

Anthropologists propose another answer: that the *Diné*, as the Navajos call themselves, came from Alaska and the Pacific Northwest to what is now the American Southwest relatively recently, between five and eight hundred years ago. They probably arrived knowing how to make excellent baskets and mats, but among the established Pueblo people they found something new: male weavers producing fine cotton fabrics on vertical looms. By about 1650 the freewheeling and eclectic Navajos had learned this craft from their neighbors, although it was adopted mostly by Navajo women rather than men. Soon afterward, Spaniards, sheep, and wool entered the Southwest and transformed Pueblo and Navajo culture, including weaving.

| NAVAJO RUG DESIGNS |

By the eighteenth century Navajo weavers were already famous, and a textile trade was well established, for their products were very distinctive. They "work their wool with more delicacy and taste than the Spaniards," admitted a colonial governor of New Mexico in 1795. "Their woolen fabrics are the most valuable in our province," wrote another Spaniard in 1812. A few decades later, American travelers marveled over the exquisite, tight weave that made Navajo textiles flexible but waterproof, even water-tight. They were also highly prized by other Native Americans as far away as western Canada, the Great Plains, and the Great Lakes.

At this point the Navajos wove blankets, soft and drapeable, which were used as bedding, saddle blankets, wraps, and lighter clothing. Pairs of them, sewed together, formed women's dresses, called *bííls*. Besides being technically proficient,

Bitagu–Lichi–Bitzi wearing a traditional dress, 1910. E. A. Burbank, oil on canvas.

ERAS OF NAVAJO WEAVING

Specialists often divide the history of Navajo textiles into several periods.
All dates are approximate.

CLASSIC PERIOD (1650–1865)
Fine shoulder blankets, women's dresses, and serape styles. Striped or banded designs, possibly influenced by earlier basketry patterns, in mainly white, brown, black, red, and blue handspun wool.

TRANSITION PERIOD (1865–1895)
Blankets and serapes, followed by early floor rugs and other textiles for Euro-American market. Striped, banded, geometric, or strong overall designs, becoming highly inventive, complex patterns often utilizing commercial dyes, yarns, and cloth in "eyedazzler" patterns and colors. Dye, trade cloth, and yarn, especially from Germantown, Pennsylvania, in many bold colors, along with native wool. Some loss of technical quality.

RUG PERIOD (1895–1940)
Rugs and specialty textiles for the new tourist and export markets. Trading post era. Regional specialization, bordered floor-oriented patterns, influence of Oriental rug designs, many new inventions as well as revivals of classic styles, including J. L. Hubbell's campaign at Ganado. Wide range of yarns and dyes, with attention to weaving quality and to marketing.

RECENT PERIOD (1940–PRESENT)
Rugs and new tapestries intended for wall display, as well as round and tufted weavings. Regional styles become general, showing continued innovation along with increased professionalism among weavers.

Navajo weavers were creative, eclectic, and quite willing to experiment. Traditional Pueblo textiles were woven wider side-to-side than long, while Spanish serapes and ponchos, as well as bed blankets, were woven longer than wide. Navajo weavers adopted both styles and soared beyond them.

Like their Pueblo models, early Navajo blankets were borderless and striped, which still allowed for many subtle variations of design. A nineteenth-century explorer said that the blankets on the backs of the Diné reminded him of stratified layers of rocks, and in fact blanket colors were limited to earthy natural wool tones, with two exceptions. Blue yarn was dyed with indigo from Mexico, and trade with the outside world also provided a scarlet woolen fabric known as *bayeta*, which could be patiently unraveled and respun to make red yarn. Spanish and Mexican serapes suggested variations on stripes, too, such as zigzags, terrace patterns, diamonds, serrations, and occasionally a large central element in the pattern.

As the nineteenth century progressed, more and more outsiders came west, carrying their goods with them, and Navajos wove these

IN DESIGN AND WEAVE IT IS A WONDERFULLY SUPERIOR PIECE OF WORK. I DOUBT IF A FINER PIECE OF NAVAHO WEAVING ... HAS EVER BEEN SEEN.

—GEORGE WHARTON JAMES, TRAVEL WRITER

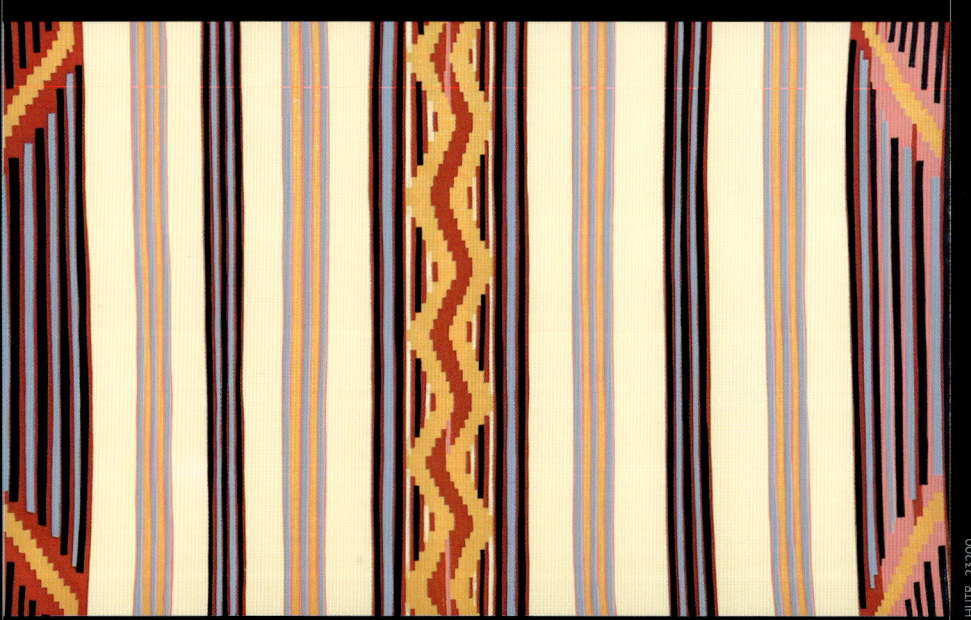

NAVAJO RUG DESIGNS

NAVAJO RUG DESIGNS

— 26 —

changes into their blankets. The biggest upheaval in their history occurred between 1864 and 1868, when the U.S. Army rounded up and imprisoned some eight thousand Navajos at Bosque Redondo in northwestern New Mexico. This tragic episode, known as the Long Walk, brought nearly the entire population into contact with Euro-American culture, and when the survivors were finally allowed to walk home they had begun to wear commercial cloth and to use machine-made blankets. The classic Navajo blanket was on its way to becoming a rug.

Railroads reached the Southwest in the 1880s, greatly increasing Navajo exposure to the habits, goods, and evils of the wider world. Trading posts—licensed stores operated by non-Indians both on and near reservations—also served as cultural crossroads. Merchants like Juan Lorenzo Hubbell traded such products as flour, sugar, tools, and cloth for Navajo wool, livestock, pine nuts, and blankets. But how were traders to find buyers for these handsome handmade weavings? Other than as curios, how could Anglo-Americans use them?

Wild West shows, dime novels, the Chicago Exposition of 1893, and several famous anthropological expeditions had fanned

NAVAJO RUG DESIGNS

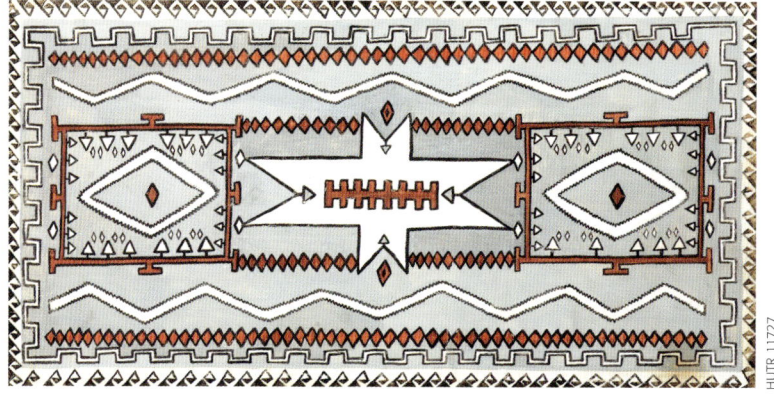

public interest in the frontier. Railroads made travel quicker and easier, and tourist services provided by the new Fred Harvey Company made it almost comfortable. Railroads also made mail-order businesses possible. Hubbell, like many others of his

time, probably feared that Native Americans were doomed unless they could adapt to the modern world. Certainly he shook his head over what he saw as a decline in the quality of Navajo weaving—in a rush to produce blankets, which were often sold in the American market by the pound, some weavers cut corners. "Cheap and gaudy blankets, loosely put together—made here, there, and everywhere—have been sold at fabulous prices," wrote Hubbell in his 1902 catalogue. "[But] I have been at the greatest pains to perpetuate the old patterns, colors, and weaves.… I can guarantee the reproduction of these ancient patterns."

In the fall of 1897 a young artist named E. A. Burbank arrived at the Hubbell Trading Post. After training in Chicago and Munich he had recently set out on what became a lifelong mission to paint pictures of Native Americans, beginning with a portrait of

Geronimo. Hubbell welcomed him and refused to charge for room and board. "I stayed," Burbank recalled in his autobiography, "but eased my conscience by presenting him with pictures, and by copying rug designs for him. Mr. Hubbell turned his office over to me for a studio."

Hubbell knew a good trade when he saw it. Here, long before color photography, was a great way to capture the weavers' sizzling colors and vigorous patterns and put them to new uses, such as

historic preservation, marketing, teaching, nonverbal communication, and his own personal pleasure. Over the years Burbank spent much time at Ganado, where the Navajos dubbed him "Many Brushes" and "One Who Puts You on a Piece of Paper." His paintings and drawings form the core of the Hubbell art collection, although he was only one of many painters, photographers, and sculptors who visited and worked there. Later Burbank remembered watching the weavers inspect his work, "studying the patterns and colors and then with their hands, measuring off the size," and then producing a rug "exactly like the picture."

"Some of the weavers contradicted this, saying they never wove from the painted rug designs," as Martha Blue points out in *Indian Trader: The Life and Times of J. L. Hubbell.* Insights offered by modern weavers suggest that once again there is no clear-cut answer, only a dynamic creative process at work. A contemporary textile scholar, Ann Lane Hedlund, observes that when Navajo weavers are asked about other weavers' work, the typical response is, "It's up to her." Modern inspirations for weavers include books and magazines

NAVAJO RUG DESIGNS

HUTR 2770

HUTR 2789

HUTR 3517

HUTR 16165

HUTR 23208

HUTR 2765

— 32 —

| NAVAJO RUG DESIGNS |

> WEAVING IS PART OF ART.
> INSTEAD OF HOLDING THE PAINTBRUSH,
> YOU USE YARN AND WOOL.
>
> —LARRY YAZZIE, WEAVER, TUBA CITY/COAL MINE MESA, ARIZONA

as well as family traditions, but Hedlund aptly describes the usual design as "an original hybrid" and quotes an anonymous weaver on her work: "From head to toe you are saturated with weaving. You are thinking, 'How am I going to design it?' Everything is put into weaving a rug.... It seems like you are selling your mind." (For other fascinating glimpses of weavers at work, see Hedlund's *Reflections of the Weaver's World*.)

NAVAJO RUG DESIGNS

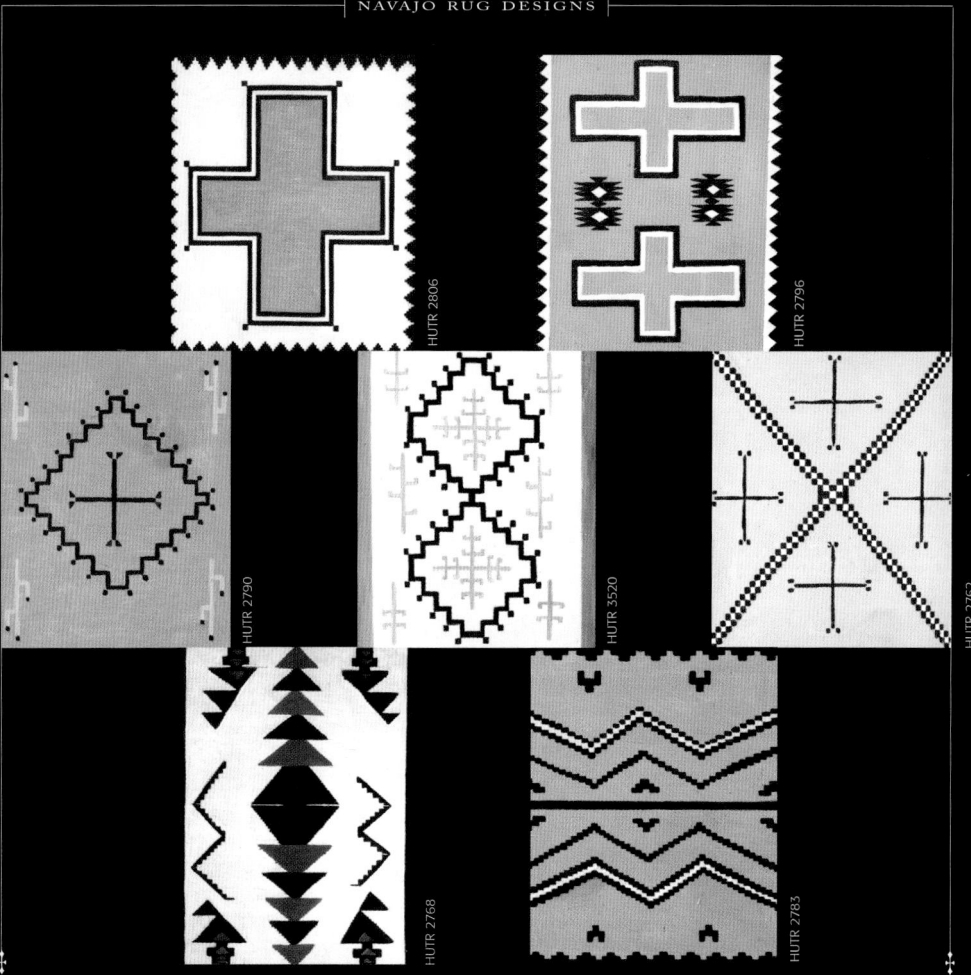

| NAVAJO RUG DESIGNS |

THE BEAUTY OF A GENUINE NAVAJO BLANKET IS ITS SIMPLICITY
OF DESIGN AND HARMONY OF COLOR.

—E. A. BURBANK, ARTIST

| NAVAJO RUG DESIGNS |

Almost nothing is known about the talented painter Bertha Little, except that she taught briefly at the Presbyterian College at Ganado. In an unpublished manuscript, Martha Blue quotes a letter from Little to Hubbell that reveals "an aura of secrecy" surrounding her rug paintings. Hubbell lent her weavings to copy but seems to have stipulated that nobody except the artist should see them. Apparently concerned about competition from rival weavers and traders, he also refused to publish any of the rug designs as cards.

| NAVAJO RUG DESIGNS |

He did have rivals. In 1896 Hubbell's former partner, C. N. Cotton, had issued a *Wholesale Catalogue and Price List of Navajo Blankets*, designed, written, and printed by George Wharton James. Between 1903 and 1911 J. B. Moore, the trader at Crystal, New Mexico, published three. Both included color plates, and like Hubbell promoted the use of the weavings as rugs. Moore apparently showed the weavers Oriental rug patterns as models. "No design of blanket in this book can be reproduced," Cotton warned, while Moore's disclaimer read: "Each and every individual piece will be found more or less different from all others." Thanks to the merchandising efforts of traders, the Fred Harvey Company (Hubbell's largest customer), and

art dealers from Pasadena to New York, Navajo rugs became fashionable. Across America they adorned floors, walls, piano benches, and baby carriages, and they proved especially popular as décor in the "great camps" of the Adirondacks, including Theodore Roosevelt's summer home.

Of the other rug-design artists, Hardesty Maratta, another Chicagoan, was also a printer and produced the Hubbell letterhead. Raymond Pearson's three large paintings date from 1935, when Hubbell's sons were running the post. Waldo Mootzka was a Hopi artist, which explains the presence of the exquisite black and white plaid design, a Hopi boy's blanket, among the Navajo textiles (HUTR 11719). H. B. Judy came from Brooklyn, accompanying an ethnologist and curator from the Brooklyn Museum named Stewart Culin.

> Every day she cards wool,
> Releasing aromas of wet lambs. . . .
> > She soaks wool in the eyes of spider woman,
> > The weaver of creation, weaving together
> > Brown, yellow, black, white and red—
> > Shade of her soul-self.
> >
> > —From "Spider Woman's Children" by Hershman John

| NAVAJO RUG DESIGNS |

The unsigned works probably include some by a mysterious Miss Bonsall, who is mentioned in the Hubbell letters, as well as at least one more Burbank (HUTR 3527). Some of the original rug studies are known to be lost, which isn't surprising. Hubbell seems to have lent them out like library books.

And they can be read. They're a nonverbal but brilliant guide to Navajo textiles at the moment of transformation from blankets into

NAVAJO RUG DESIGNS

NAVAJO RUG DESIGNS

> WEAVING TAKES A LOT OF CAREFUL THINKING. IT'S ALL I
> THINK ABOUT WHEN I'M WORKING. IT TAKES CAREFUL MEASURING
> TOO.... AND YOU MUST MEASURE OVER AND OVER AGAIN AS YOU PUT
> IN THE PATTERNS SO THAT THEY COME OUT EVEN. IF IT DOESN'T COME
> OUT RIGHT, YOU TAKE IT OUT AND MEASURE AGAIN.... I DON'T MAKE
> MY RUGS CHEAPLY—A LOT OF HARD WORK IS INVOLVED.
>
> —MARY H. (LEE) BEGAY, WEAVER, GANADO, ARIZONA

rugs. To represent the past, here are traditional women's dresses of indigo blue with red borders and several kinds of shoulder blanket, including dark-bordered, Pueblo-inspired *mantas*; Spanish- and Mexican-influenced serapes and ponchos; and many horizontally striped chief's blankets. One of these designs (HUTR 2781) also appears in Hubbell's 1902 catalogue labeled "Hanolchadi or chief's blanket. Very oldest pattern known" and priced from $17.50 to $25.00.

To put these prices in perspective, consider that a contemporary Montgomery Ward catalogue advertised a girl's cotton dress for 90 cents and a boy's three-piece suit for $2.50. An ordinary rug cost $5, while an upright piano sold for $100. Good Navajo weavings have never been cheap.

Looking to the future, red, black, gray, and white designs clearly herald the birth of the famous Ganado Red rugs, known for central double crosses, which are definitely non-Christian in this context, or variations on diamonds. Swastika patterns, such as the one in HUTR 2764, deserve special mention. This traditional Native American symbol is a sure way to date a design: though once common, it has not appeared in Navajo weaving since World War II, when Navajo soldiers greatly distinguished themselves as Code Talkers. Bordered or framed patterns, such as HUTR 2777, have clearly crossed the line from wearing blanket to floor rug. As always among Navajo weavings, here are practical saddle blankets (HUTR 3517), as well as some early *ye'ii* or figurative weavings (HUTR 11726). Curiously, HUTR 2807 and HUTR 3528 are very similar, but Burbank labeled them "No. 21" and "No. 22."

And what about those daughter and granddaughter rugs? Like human heredity, artistic inheritance is unpredictable, sometimes almost magical. The countless descendants of these designs range from close relatives to mere kissing cousins. Only a few are copies. For example, in 1981 Mary H. Begay (formerly Mary Lee Begay) wove an exact replica of Bertha Little's double red crosses (HUTR

 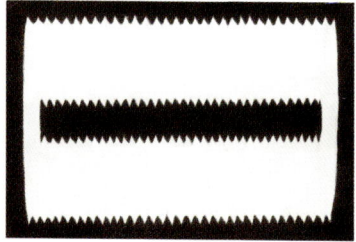

NAVAJO RUG DESIGNS

HUTR 2798

HUTR 2809

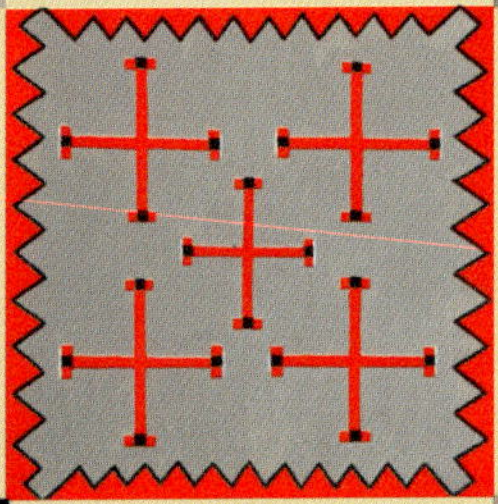

HUTR 2761

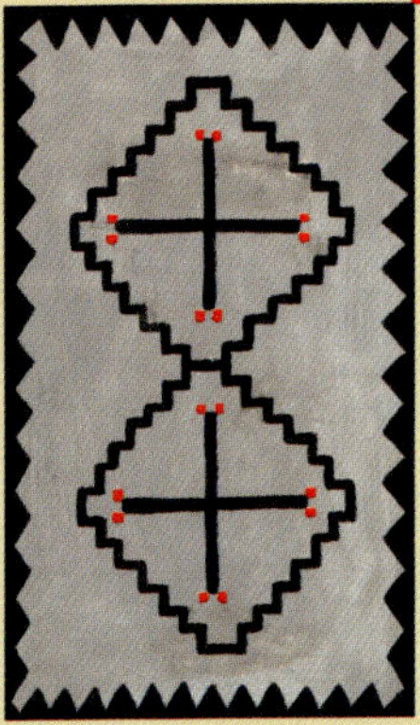

HUTR 2769

HUTR 2801

— 50 —

NAVAJO RUG DESIGNS

> WEAVING TAKES YOUR WHOLE HEAD. YOU NEED TO KNOW SCIENCE AND MATH, ESPECIALLY ALGEBRA AND GEOMETRY. IRENE'S DESIGNS ARE OUTRAGEOUS. OUR MOTHER SAYS THAT SHE OUTDESIGNS EVEN HER. SOME OF THESE WEAVERS, LIKE MY SISTER, ARE REAL PROFESSIONALS.
>
> —MARIA SALTCLAW, SISTER OF IRENE CLARK, WEAVER, CRYSTAL, NEW MEXICO

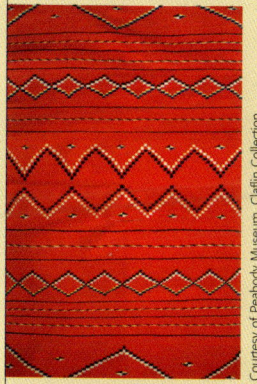

Courtesy of Peabody Museum, Claflin Collection

HUTR 3524

Courtesy of Maxwell Museum

2792), which now belongs to the Denver Art Museum (see below). And there are three known variants of Burbank's "No. 9" (HUTR 3524, a beautiful bayeta serape): the possible model for the painting, located in the Maxwell Museum of Archaeology in Albuquerque; a remarkable all-silk version that belongs to the University of Colorado Museum in Boulder; and a woolen copy in the Claflin Collection at Harvard's Peabody Museum (see page 51).

When he acquired his serape in the 1930s, William Claflin also collected its story, which Laurie Webster tells in *Collecting the*

Bertha Little's painting (left) and Mary H. (Lee) Begay's rug (right).

NAVAJO RUG DESIGNS

Weaver's Art. In the 1890s, looking for models to inspire weavers and to keep the bayeta tradition alive, Juan Lorenzo Hubbell borrowed a rare old bayeta blanket and had three copies made (or maybe four, including Burbank's painting). The oldest blanket is the one in Albuquerque, and it probably did inspire the others. But close inspection reveals that the four designs are not quadruplicates; they vary in many small details. The Claflin rug supposedly hung on the wall of the Hubbell Trading post until 1923, when Hubbell used it as collateral for a loan—and lost it to the lender, from whom Claflin bought it for $150.

| NAVAJO RUG DESIGNS |

HUTR 3515

HUTR 2760

HUTR 2755

HUTR 2764

HUTR 2803

NAVAJO RUG DESIGNS

HUTR 2793

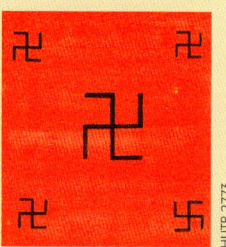
HUTR 2773

HUTR 2777

| NAVAJO RUG DESIGNS |

It's also interesting to compare the rug designs in the paintings with the thirteen weavings displayed in a much-published photograph made by Ben Wittick (see page 9) at the Hubbell Trading Post around 1890. In the foreground a young weaver shows her chief-style rug to Hubbell and her husband. In the background hang a collection of chief blankets, serapes, and rugs with large double motifs—original hybrids of the painted rug designs.

Or is it vice versa? There are no simple answers, but Navajo weaving continues on its dynamic way. For at least 150 years, observers have been lamenting its decline and fall: the good weavers are passing away; the really fine work is lost and gone. These are the same voices that probably lamented, when the first blankets came off the looms centuries ago, that they were too expensive, and the ancient bark mats were so much better made! Yet reliable sources estimate that the number of active weavers among the quarter of a million contemporary Navajos is approximately 30,000. This book, which looks hopefully forward as well as back into the past, is dedicated to them.

ABOVE: *H. B. Judy, c. 1905.*

RUG DESIGNS BY HUTR NUMBERS

HUTR 2325
Oil on canvas, 19.2 x 24.2 cm
E. A. Burbank (American, 1858-1949)

HUTR 2755
Oil on canvas, 29.1 x 24.1 cm
Artist unknown

HUTR 2756
Oil on plywood, 45.7 x 30.5 cm
Artist unknown

HUTR 2757
Oil on canvas, 19 x 24.3 cm
E. A. Burbank

HUTR 2758
Oil on canvas, 24.4 x 19.2 cm
E. A. Burbank

HUTR 2759
Oil on canvas, 20.9 x 27.2 cm
Bertha Little (American? Dates unknown)

HUTR 2760
Oil on canvas, 22.1 x 29.7 cm
Bertha Little

HUTR 2761
Oil on canvas, 24.6 x 24.5 cm
Bertha Little

HUTR 2762
Oil on canvas, 31.1 x 25.2 cm
Artist unknown

HUTR 2763
Ink and watercolor on fiiber board, 12 x 21.8 cm
H. G. Maratta (American, 1864-1924)

HUTR 2764
Oil on canvas, 20.4 x 26.9 cm
E. A. Burbank

HUTR 2765
Ink and gouache, 12 x 18 cm
H. G. Maratta

HUTR 2766
Oil on canvas, 29.8 x 24.5 cm
Bertha Little

HUTR 2767
Oil on canvas, 19.3 x 24.3 cm
E. A. Burbank

HUTR 2768
Oil on canvas, 20.4 x 26.8 cm
E. A. Burbank

HUTR 2769
Oil on canvas, 18.2 x 27.1 cm
E. A. Burbank

HUTR 2770
Oil on canvas, 29.7 x 23.3 cm
Artist unknown

HUTR 2771
Oil on canvas, 21.5 x 14.5 cm
Artist unknown

HUTR 2772
Oil on canvas, 19.6 x 24.5 cm
Bertha Little

HUTR 2773
Watercolor on paper, 32.9 x 30.1 cm
H. B. Judy (or Tschudy, American, 1874-1946)

HUTR 2774
Oil on canvas, 21.9 x 29.8 cm
Artist unknown

HUTR 2775
Oil on canvas, 20.4 x 26.8 cm
E. A. Burbank

HUTR 2776
Oil on canvas, 19.2 x 24.3 cm
H. G. Maratta

HUTR 2777
Oil on canvas, 20.3 x 26.8 cm
E. A. Burbank

HUTR 2778
Oil on canvas, 19.3 x 24.3 cm
E. A. Burbank

HUTR 2779
Oil on canvas, 22 x 29.7 cm
Bertha Little

HUTR 2780
Oil on canvas, 19.4 x 24.4 cm
E. A. Burbank

HUTR 2781
Oil on canvas, 19.4 x 24.5 cm
E. A. Burbank

HUTR 2782
Oil on canvas, 29.8 x 22 cm
Bertha Little

HUTR 2783
Oil on canvas, 29. 2 x 18 cm
E. A. Burbank

NAVAJO RUG DESIGNS

HUTR 2784
Watercolor on paper,
12 x 24.5 cm
Artist unknown
Same design as HUTR 16166.

HUTR 2785
Oil on canvas, 18.4 x 27.2 cm
Bertha Little

HUTR 2786
Gouache on fiiber board,
10.2 x 20.5 cm
H. G. Maratta

HUTR 2787
Oil on canvas, 27.1 x 20.6
Bertha Little

HUTR 2788
Oil on canvas, 19.2 x 24.5 cm
E. A. Burbank

HUTR 2789
Oil on canvas, 22 x 29.8 cm
Bertha Little

HUTR 2790
Oil on canvas, 29.2 x 17.5 cm
E. A. Burbank

HUTR 2791
Oil on canvas, 19.3 x 24.4 cm
E. A. Burbank

HUTR 2792
Oil on canvas, 18.1 x 27.2 cm
Bertha Little

HUTR 2793
Oil on canvas, 22.2 x 25.7 cm
Bertha Little

HUTR 2794
Watercolor on paper,
11.6 x 14.4 cm
Artist unknown

HUTR 2795
Oil on canvas, 26.9 x 20.5
E. A. Burbank

HUTR 2796
Oil on canvas, 28 x 23.3 cm
Artist unknown

HUTR 2797
Color photographic print of lost rug design
Oil on canvas, 20.3 x 25.2 cm
E. A. Burbank

HUTR 2798
Oil on canvas, 29.8 x 24.4 cm
Artist unknown

HUTR 2799
Oil on canvas, 22 x 25.7 cm
Bertha Little

HUTR 2800
Oil on canvas, 19.2 x 24.4 cm
E. A. Burbank

HUTR 2801
Oil on canvas, 28.5 x 18.3 cm
Artist unknown

HUTR 2802
Oil on canvas, 21.9 x 29.2 cm
Artist unknown

HUTR 2803
Oil on canvas, 20.3 x 26.8 cm
E. A. Burbank

HUTR 2804
Oil on canvas, 22 x 29.8 cm
Bertha Little

HUTR 2805
Oil on canvas, 19.3 x 24.3 cm
E. A. Burbank

HUTR 2806
Oil on canvas, 22 x 25.9 cm
Bertha Little

HUTR 2807
Oil on canvas, 19.2 x 24.3 cm
E. A. Burbank

HUTR 2808
Oil on canvas, 20.5 x 26.9 cm
Artist unknown

HUTR 2809
Oil on canvas, 20.4 x 26.8 cm
Bertha Little

HUTR 2810
Oil on canvas, 29.8 x 22.1 cm
Artist unknown

HUTR 2811
Oil on canvas, 24.3 x 19.1
E. A. Burbank

HUTR 2812
Watercolor on paper,
53.7 x 42.1 cm
Artist unknown

HUTR 2813
Oil on canvas, 51 x 76.5 cm
Artist unknown

HUTR 3514
Oil on canvas, 21.5 x 27.4 cm
Artist unknown

NAVAJO RUG DESIGNS

HUTR 3515
Oil on canvas, 21.5 x 28 cm
E. A. Burbank

HUTR 3516
Oil on pebble board,
19 x 28.1 cm
Artist unknown

HUTR 3517
Oil on canvas, 19.3 x 24.4 cm
E. A. Burbank

HUTR 3518
Oil on canvas, 21.5 x 28.2 cm
E. A. Burbank

HUTR 3519
Oil on canvas, 20 x 24.6 cm
E. A. Burbank

HUTR 3520
Oil on canvas, 20.7 x 29.1 cm
Artist unknown

HUTR 3521
Oil on canvas, 19.3 x 24.4 cm
E. A. Burbank
Note on back: "This design was made by a Moqui [Hopi] Indian."

HUTR 3522
Oil on canvas, 20.6 x 30.9 cm
Bertha Little

HUTR 3523
Oil on canvas, 24.6 x 34.6 cm
Bertha Little

HUTR 3524
Oil on canvas, 19.3 x 24.4 cm
E. A. Burbank

HUTR 3525
Oil on canvas, 19.2 x 24.3 cm
E. A. Burbank

HUTR 3526
Oil on canvas, 19.2 x 24.5 cm
E. A. Burbank

HUTR 3527
Oil on canvas, 19.3 x 24.4 cm
Attributed to E. A. Burbank

HUTR 3528
Oil on canvas, 19.2 x 24.4 cm
E. A. Burbank

HUTR 3529
Oil on canvas, 19.3 x 24.4 cm
E. A. Burbank

HUTR 4227
Oil on canvas, 20.2 x 27.9 cm
Artist unknown

HUTR 11717
Watercolor on paper, 27.7 x 21.3 cm
Artist unknown

HUTR 11718
Crayon on paper, 27.7 x 21.3 cm
Artist unknown

HUTR 11719
Tempera on paper, 41.7 x 27.1 cm
Waldo Mootzka (Hopi,
1903-1940)

HUTR 11720
Tempera on paper, 41.7 x 27.1 cm
Attributed to Waldo Mootzka

HUTR 11726
Tempera on paper, 35.7 x 44 cm
Raymond Pearson (American?
Dates unknown)

HUTR 11727
Tempera on paper,
49.5 x 25.5 cm
Attributed to Raymond Pearson

HUTR 11728
Tempera on paper, 35.5 x 48 cm,
Raymond Pearson

HUTR 11731
Oil on plywood, 9.6 x 14.8 cm
Artist unknown

HUTR 16165
Oil on paper, 28 x 35.3 cm
Artist unknown

HUTR 16166
Tempera on paper,
44.5 x 30.2 cm
Artist unknown. Same design
as HUTR 2784.

HUTR 16167
Color photographic print,
42 x 27.6 cm
Artist unknown

HUTR 23198-23212
Silkscreen prints, 66.4 x 50.8 cm
Louis Ewing (American,
1908-1983)

RECOMMENDED READING

Amsden, Charles Avery. *Navaho Weaving: Its Technic and Its History.* Santa Ana, CA: The Fine Arts Press, 1934.

Blue, Martha. *Indian Trader: The Life and Times of J. L. Hubbell.* Walnut, CA: Kiva Publishing, 2000.

Cheek, Lawrence W. *The Navajo Long Walk.* Tucson, AZ: Rio Nuevo Publishers, 2004.

Hedlund, Ann Lane. *Reflections of the Weaver's World: The Gloria F. Ross Collection of Contemporary Navajo Weaving.* Denver, CO: Denver Art Museum, 1992.

Kaufman, Alice, and Christopher Selser. *The Navajo Weaving Tradition: 1650 to the Present.* New York: Dutton, 1985.

Kent, Kate Peck. *Navajo Weaving: Three Centuries of Change.* Santa Fe, NM: School of American Research Press, 1985.

McManis, Kent, and Robert Jeffries. *A Guide to Navajo Weavings.* Tucson, AZ: Rio Nuevo Publishers, 1997.

Webster, Laurie D. *Collecting the Weaver's Art: The William Claflin Collection of Southwestern Textiles.* Cambridge, MA: Peabody Museum Press, Harvard University, 2003.

SOURCES AND CREDITS

Hubbell Trading Post images on pp. 1, 2-3, and 5: HUTR 3516, HUTR 2763, and HUTR 4227. Image on p. 51 (lower left) courtesy of Peabody Museum, Harvard University Photo T906; image on p. 51 (lower right) courtesy of Maxwell Museum of Anthropology, University of New Mexico, catalogue number 63.34.151; image on p. 52 (lower right) 1981 Hubbell Revival rug weaving by Mary H. (Lee) Begay, Denver Art Museum Collection: Gloria F. Ross Collection, 1981.113, © Mary H. (Lee) Begay, photo courtesy of Denver Art Museum. George Wharton James quote on p. 24: from James, George Wharton, *Indian Blankets and Their Makers* (Chicago: A. C. McClurg & Co., 1914), p. 47. Larry Yazzie quote on p. 33, Grace Henderson Nez quote on p. 41, Mary H. (Lee) Begay quote on p. 47, and Maria Saltclaw quote on p. 51: from Hedlund, Ann Lane, *Reflections of the Weaver's World: The Gloria*

F. Ross Collection of Contemporary Navajo Weaving (Denver, CO: Denver Art Museum, 1992), pp. 104, 28, 30, and 61. E. A. Burbank quote on p. 39: from Burbank, E. A., and Ernest Royce, *Burbank among the Indians* (Caldwell, ID: Caxton Printers, 1946), p. 55. Lines from "Spider Woman's Children," p. 44: from John, Hershman, "Spider Woman's Children," *Journal of Navajo Education* XIV (1996–97), p. 3; also at www.applehollow.com/spiderwoman.html. Sierra Ornelas quote (below): exhibit label in Navajo Weaving at Arizona State Museum: 19th Century Blankets, 20th Century Rugs, 21st Century Views, 2004–2005.

> MY GRANDMOTHER VALUES WHETHER HER GRANDKIDS ARE WEAVING OR NOT. YOU COULD TELL HER, "HEY, I JUST GOT A JOB AT NASA AS AN ASTRONAUT AND I'M GOING TO THE MOON." AND SHE WOULD SAY, "THAT'S NICE, ARE YOU WEAVING?" SHE UNDERSTANDS THE IMPORTANCE OF CONTINUING THE TRADITION.
>
> —SIERRA ORNELAS, WEAVER, TUCSON, ARIZONA

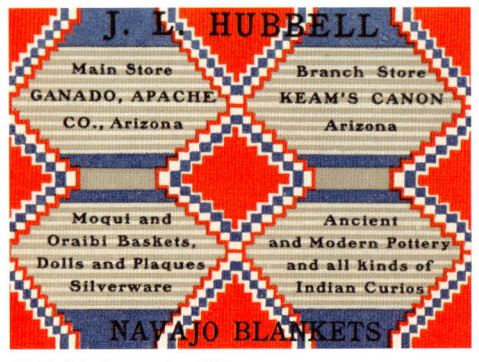

Hubbell business card, c. 1902.